In Pursuit of M
Considerations for the Improvement of Sprint Performance in the 21st Century

In Pursuit of Maximum Speed:
Considerations for the Improvement of Sprint Performance in the 21st Century
(A Guide for Youth and High School Track and Field Athletes)

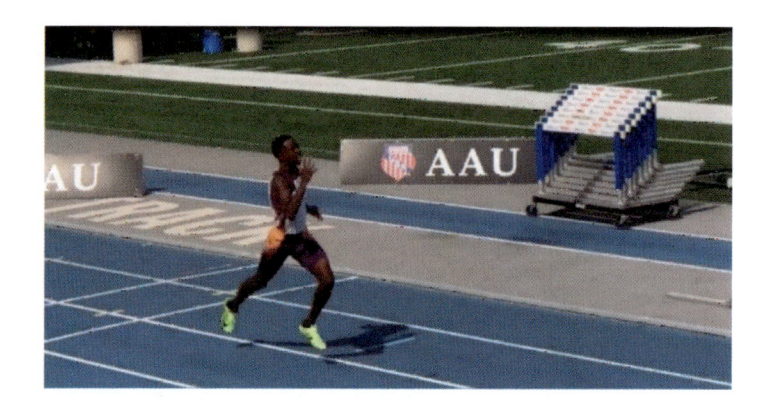

M.D. Shahid
Prof. of Chemistry

For 20 years I searched for *"The Holy Grail of Speed,"* only to find out that it was just a myth, it does not exist. In the end, maximum speed is a blend of science, hard work, and a little help from Mother Nature.

— M.D Shahid

Copyright © 2024 by Muslim Shahid
All rights reserved. Reproduction in whole
or in part is prohibited.
ISBN: 9798879950632

Contents

Preface	i
Overview	iv
I. Energy and Work	1
II. Human Metabolic Energy Systems	3
III. Speed: Skill and Physiology	5
IV. Core Factors That Affect Speed	7
V. Considerations in Training for Speed	13
VI. Phases of the Sprint Run	16
VII. Acceleration and Maximum Velocity	20
VIII. Considerations for the 400-meter Dash	23
IX. Considerations for Speed Workouts	27
X. Sample Training Sessions	29
XI. Considerations for Club	31
XII. Glossary of Definitions	33
References	37

Preface

I am a senior research scientist with an MS in chemistry, hold 49 US patents, and love the sport of track and field. As an AAU/USTAF track and field club coach for almost 30 years and a former high school track coach, I have trained and developed many youth athletes who became competitive sprinters. Four of those youths became Texas State champions. One state champion became an AAU national champion, while another later became an NCAA D1 champion and a USATF National champion. Sprinting is an anaerobic event, yet during my coaching career, I have heard many coaches and trainers tell parents that their special aerobic workouts would make their kids faster. Ironically, since the 90s, there have been numerous track and field publications that have reviewed the neurological and biomechanical factors that influence how *speed* is expressed in human locomotion. Yet, many of those who champion the sport of youth track and field appear to have no idea that this kind of information exists. Obviously, there is a void on the information highways that links the elite track and field community to the amateur community of youth track and field. This manual attempts to bridge that void and help junior-level track and field participants understand the science of *speed* and *sprint performance*.

This book is divided into sections that highlight topics on speed and speed development for sprinting. Some sections define speed and the factors influencing speed performance. There is also a section that explains the human metabolic pathways that produce the energy necessary for speed and speed development.

Other sections discuss the physiological core factors and the athletic skills that must be developed to improve sprint performance. Further sections discuss and teach proper biomechanical running techniques and specific drill sets for central nervous system (CNS) sensory motor development. Later in the manual there is a section on the 400-meter dash: aerobic vs. anaerobic training. Finally, there are sections in the book that give sample warm-up exercises and drills, training regimes for speed and speed endurance, training schedules for club and high school track coaches, a glossary, and an extensive reference listing that supports the manual's content.

Numerous hours of research were needed to source the data on the science of speed development and sprint performance presented in this manual. Even more time was necessary to digest this scientific data in order to present it in a fashion and language that would be clear to the public. The information was then formatted so that an amateur track coach or a parent could use this manual as a "how-to guide" in designing training regimes for youth athletes.

Let me be frank: I am aware that this manual falls far short of the expansive research works that have been published recently in peer-reviewed journals on the science of "sprint performance." For example, the manual only summarizes the comprehensive areas of strength development, mechanical competency, and coordination development necessary for increased sprint performance. Likewise, out of caution and safety concerns, the discussions on Olympic weightlifting for power improvements in the text is only directed to those youth athletes 14 years and older. Finally, in section VI of the manual, you will find that I am silent on how to set and use starting blocks.

Indeed, a voluminous work would be required to do justice on the subject of "speed" and "sprint performance" in the sport of track and field. Rather, the hope is that this instructional manual will be a useful tool to help guide and assist novice track participants, youth athletes, parents, club track coaches, and track and field trainers in their quest to improve overall speed and sprint performance in their youth athletes.

Overview

Contrary to popular beliefs found circulating throughout the sport of youth track and field, there is nothing *aerobic* about *sprinting*. There is nothing magical to be gained by having athletes doing 1500-meter breakdown runs in practice (e.g., 500, 400, 300, 200, 100) or repeated 800-meter or 500-meter runs that will result in increased speed improvements in your athletes. Extensive aerobic training will also not increase speed endurance in your athletes. Repeated biomechanical and neurobiological research studies combined with physiological evaluations of sprint performance over the past 30 years have proven that aerobic training does not affect speed endurance.

Sprinting is purely an *anaerobic* running event. Anaerobic metabolic energy processes produce work without the use of oxygen transport to the muscles. Consequently, aerobic training regimes should never be used to train athletes to run faster if they are in pursuit of *"maximum speed"* (Veney, 2011).

Personal trainers and sports gyms frequently use social media to promote a package of sports drills to young athletes, suggesting that their training programs will increase their speed. News flash: drills alone will not help improve your athlete's speed. Drills such as speed hurdle runs, ladder runs, and cone shuttle runs look cute, even flashy, but drills alone will do nothing to increase speed in your athlete. Specific drills will improve your athlete's CNS sensory motor responses, coordination, and center of mass, but these drills alone will not increase speed.

The truth is, if you want your athletes to run fast at competitive track meets, you should have training workouts that run them fast during practice sessions. When designing training programs, you must focus on speed and power workouts for your athletes that use submaximal/maximal runs (intensive training).

This instruction manual will cover topics such as the human metabolic energy systems, coordination, energy, work, and heat; speed: biomechanical and neurological skills needed to support fast running; sprint mechanics: dynamics, kinematics, and proper foot placement; mobility and its effect on sprint performance; CNS sensory motor development; speed: skill and physiology; training guidelines to achieve maximum speed; training guidelines for momentum and acceleration; training guidelines to achieve maximum velocity; training for the 400-meter dash; and strength-power training necessary to improve maximum speed performance in youth and high school athletes.

I. Energy and Work

What is energy? There are many mathematical equations in chemistry and physics that can be used to define energy, but for track and field purposes, we will define energy as the ***ability to do work*** (U.S. Energy Information Administration, 2022). From physics, we also have the definition of work: ***Force acting on an object over a distance*** (Elsevier, 2016).

$$(1)\ E = w + q, \text{ (where w = work, q = heat)}$$

$$(2)\ W = f \times d, \text{ (where f = force, d = distance)}$$

From equation (1), energy can be converted into a work (w) component, and thus, the more energy, the more potential for work performance. Examining equation (2), when a force (f) acts through a distance (d), work is produced. It is this factor of work (w) that humans use that allows them to move by a process we define as "locomotion" (Lacquaniti, 2012). Notice also that in equation (1), there is the component q, or heat. For example, when a person is in a stressful environment/running (doing work), most of the energy is being lost from the body in the form of heat (Sawka et al., 1993). This is a necessary requirement of human thermoregulation so that the body maintains its normal average core temperature of 98.6°F during stressful activity (Sawka et al., 1993). When energy is lost as heat (q), it does not contribute to the effort of the athlete to perform mechanical work. Since science has demonstrated that only 25% of the total energy produced through muscle contraction is used for work (Vella & Kravitz, 2004), the objective of good sprint training is to develop in athletes the ability to run as efficiently as possible to minimize further physiological losses in energy caused by inefficient body movements, weak core structure, and poor breathing habits. Research studies have shown that athletes who practice relaxed breathing techniques when running, learn efficient, coordinated hand-arm cycle movements, have strong core postures, full range hip mobility, and have had proper endurance training will physiologically realize efficient conversion of their body's energy for work when performing high-intensity sprint runs (Seagrave, 1996). During this discussion on sprinting, energy systems will be defined as those metabolic mechanisms from which the body produces and uses energy to produce work for running.

II. Human Metabolic Energy Systems

In terms of locomotion, all human energy systems contribute to running performance to some degree (Thompson, 1991). Each energy system gives specific energy values for different periods of time depending on the intensity of running. Examining how the human metabolic energy systems support the **work** requirements for *fast* running will define the type of ***dynamic*** training programs necessary to develop maximum *speed* efforts in your sprinters. There are two metabolic energy processes that cause muscle contraction in humans for the production of work: anaerobic (sub-divided systems), which is stored energy that does not require oxygen to produce work, and aerobic, an energy system that requires oxygen to produce work (Thompson, 1991). Table (1) summarizes the human energy systems and their subcomponents (Shaver, 2008).

Adenosine Triphosphate (ATP): a product of the anaerobic a-lactate system, the highest-intensity biological energy system used to produce muscle contraction. This energy output system only lasts about 7 seconds.

Adenosine Triphosphate-Creatine Phosphate A-Lactate (ATP-CP A-Lactate): an anaerobic energy process that is the next highest-intensity energy system. The duration output is about 30 seconds, much longer than the A-lactate ATP output system.

Anaerobic Lactate (ANL): a part of the ATP-CP system providing a final burst of energy (about three seconds) before lactate levels in the muscles increase dramatically.

Aerobics (AER): Though its metabolic pathways are slow, and the energy output intensity is low, the aerobic energy system is very efficient and thus extremely useful for extended periods of running.

Table (1)
Human Energy Systems

	ATP Energy System	ATP-CP Energy System	Lactic Acid Energy System	Aerobic Energy System
Chemical Basis	Anaerobic A-Lactate	Anaerobic A-Lactate	Lactate system	Aerobic glycolytic system
Origin of Energy Source	Mitochondria anaerobic expression	Skeletal muscular System	Anaerobic glycolysis	Fats and glycogen storage
Duration Period	7 seconds	30 seconds	3 seconds	2-hr plus
Biological Expression	Instant chemical reaction, but short	Fast chemical reactions, much slower than mitochondria	Moderate reaction rate, complex, short	Slow, complex chemical reactions
Metabolic Reaction By Products	Inorganic Phosphate ADP	Inorganic Phosphate ADP	Lactate Acid H protons ADP	CO_2 H_2O

III. Speed: Skill and Physiology

Speed is the ability of the neuromuscular system to produce the greatest possible impulse in the shortest possible time through a specified distance (Settle, 2014). Speed is a trainable neuromechanical component of human locomotion that is composed of many neuromuscular-neurobiological skeletal traits inherited by all humans and will vary individually from person to person (Thorson, 2018). Attempting to define thoroughly inherited speed traits or "speed potential" in any individual is beyond this manual's intent and scope. It is sufficient to say that the dominant inherited factors that will influence a person's speed potential can be traced to the individual's (1) muscle-mass/body-fat ratio distribution (Barr, 2014), (2) trunk-length considerations (Tottori et al., 2021), and (3) fast-twitch muscle fibers content (Trappe et al., 2015). Regardless of height, athletes with high muscle mass and lower body fat count will have better sprint performances overall (Barr, 2014). Current research studies also suggest that the cross-sectional areas of the trunk and the lower limb muscles, like the psoas major and the gluteus maximus, are specific muscles necessary to achieve exceptional sprint performances (Tottori et al., 2021). Finally, all humans have a genetically inherited percentage of super-fast-twitch muscle fibers (MCH IIx), fast-twitch muscle fibers (MCH IIa), and slow-twitch muscle fibers (MCH I) for doing mechanical work (Trappe et al., 2015). In running, humans use super-fast-twitch and fast-twitch muscle fibers for explosive movements and fast short runs. Slow-twitch muscle fibers are used for medium and long-distance running. In theory, individuals whose total muscle fiber content is composed of at least 71% fast-twitch fibers (including MCH IIa/MCH I hybrid fibers) can be competitive sprinters in track and field (Trappe et al., 2015).

Not having a high percentage of super-fast-twitch muscles does not mean that an athlete cannot be trained to run faster. Science has demonstrated that speed is a trainable skill (Barr, 2014). Speed depends on two elements of human locomotion: *stride length and stride frequency*. At least one of these elements must be increased to improve speed (Young, 2007). Don't waste time trying to train athletes to increase their stride length. This will generally lead to poor mechanical runs and a decrease in maximum velocity outputs by your athletes (Francis et al., 2011). Instead develop calisthenics and strength training programs for your athletes. Over time these calisthenics and strength exercises will lead to power gains by your athletes. The strength developed by your athletes will give them the ability to apply greater force-application to the ground, lowering ground contact times, resulting in both stride length and stride frequency increases (Young, 2013).

IV. Core Factors That Affect Speed

There are six fundamental biomechanical and neuromechanical factors that affect the expression of speed in human locomotion.

a. Power

Power is the force application through a distance in minimum time (Kiitta, 2019b).

$$[\text{Power} = \text{force} \times \text{distance}/\text{time}]$$

Increases in power output will result in greater force application to the ground. Increased forces will decrease ground contact times, increasing your athlete's speed. Light to moderate resistance training is an excellent means to improve power output performance (Chavez, 2023). Increase the power output in youth athletes by having them run steep inclined hills (40 meters), do 40-meter runs pulling weighted sleds, medicine ball jump and throw exercises, lunge jumps, standing broad jumps, dumbbell squats, and do low-impact plyometric jumps (See section VI for youth 14 and older).

b. Sprint Mechanics

Sprint mechanics is the dynamics and kinematics of the human motion expressed in a moving frame of reference when running (Stergiou et al., 2016). Efficient sprint mechanics begins by teaching your athletes the importance of tightening their abdomen and glute muscles while running (Seagrave, 2011). This core stabilization technique will cause the hips to extend forward, positioning them into proper running posture. Running can be segmented into two cycles (Brown & Vescovi, 2012): (1) the support phase, where one foot is planted firmly on the ground, and (2) the flight phase, where the other foot is in the air with the ankle dorsiflexed, passes directly over the knee of the planted foot, and drives straight down, striking the ground under the body's center of mass, directly under the hips (Young, 2013). During maximal velocity runs, the hips should never be positioned behind the runner's foot when it strikes the ground. This technique of "stepping over the opposite knee and driving down" will create higher knee lift in your athletes and result in shorter ground contact times (Thomas 2014; Fletcher, 2008).

Have your athletes perform repetitive maximal velocity runs from 30 to 80 meters while executing the "step over the opposite knee and drive down" technique while using their glutes and abdominal muscles for core stabilization. The motion of your athlete's arms during sprinting is rapid straight-line full-range, with fingertips moving from hip to cheek (the thumb should just reach the tip of the nose) (Fletcher, 2008; Francis et al., 2011). Consistent practice of these techniques over time will help your athletes develop proper front-side sprint mechanics, minimize backside-swing leg flops, decrease foot-ground contact time, eliminate over-striding, and reduce "swimming" (crossing the arms across the chest) (Seagrave et al., 2011).

c. Central Nervous System

The central nervous system (CNS) is where sensory impulses are transmitted, which coordinate motor skill activity (Quaal, 2019). The CNS can produce quick and powerful skillful movements in athletes, but only if the brain considers the movement safe (Smith, 2019). If the brain senses that damage or injury may occur to the body due to an unusual body movement, it will automatically down-regulate the power output to those muscle groups involved in the activity.

Efficient CNS sensory motor responses that will allow greater power output to the muscles needed for sprinting can be improved by having your athletes do circuits of (1) quick repetitions of deep vertical jumps, lunge jumps, medicine ball throws, hurdle hops, speed-hurdle run drills, weighted sled pulls, dumbbell squats with supramaximal repetitions, jump rope exercises, high-velocity Olympic weightlifting exercises (not for youth under age 14), and (2) by developing a high range of mobility and strength that will sustain high velocity running while minimizing the potential for injury (Smith, 2019).

d. Mobility/Core Strength

Athletes must develop strong core frames and an adequate range of mobility in their limbs if they are to benefit from CNS training (Hiserman, 2009). Mobility is defined as the movement of the limbs through a maximum range of motion with minimum resistance (Teichman, 2021). Mobility is essential to high sprint performance, and athletes who suffer from restrictive limb range motion will never reach their maximum velocity potential. Stiffness in the hip-joint areas and a lack of range of motion in the lower body extremities are all indications of a deficiency in the mobility of an athlete and could lead to injury.

Increased mobility and improved sprint performances can be achieved through regular practice of basic core calisthenics. Integrate these calisthenics along with your warm-up exercises before practice sessions. It is recommended that two months of mobility exercises be scheduled with your athlete's off-season conditioning program during the precompetitive track season. Examples include gorilla walks, inchworms, bear crawls, tinman, froggers, crab walks, and groin walks. Perform each of these calisthenics skills, going forward and backward. In time, your athletes will increase their hip flexibility and their range of limb mobility.

e. Coordination

Coordination is the ability to express controlled motor responses while maintaining a stable center of mass (COM) (Yang et al., 2009). Coordination is a skill that requires practice. However, with proper training your athletes will quickly begin to exhibit managed neuromuscular ability. Youth athletes grow and mature at different rates so when developing training programs make sure that you keep this under consideration. Develop your athletes coordination using air inflatable step platforms (one-leg and two-leg drills), one-leg front-back hops and maze hop drills (speed hurdles), lunge walks, alternating leg bound skips and jumps, a-b-c skip drills, fast leg drills, and jump rope exercises combined with core workouts will correct instability in COM (Osar, 2015) and result in proper body posture necessary for fast running.

f. Endurance

The capacity of an athlete to sustain high-speed runs for extended periods is called endurance (Ava, 2011). When designing speed endurance workouts, always allow for proper recovery between runs (see Section V.) Occasionally, you may want to combine speed training sessions with speed endurance sessions due to time constraints. When you combine speed and speed endurance sessions, work from the longest sprint distance to the shortest distance. This approach will help minimize injury when your athletes begin to fatigue. For short sprinting (100m/200m dash), speed endurance training sessions at submaximal/maximal intensities of 80 to 200-meters are the ideal model. For the long sprint (400m), training regimes from 200 to 350 meters at submaximal/maximal intensities will allow your athletes to improve lactate tolerance and resist CNS fatigue. However, refrain from sprint training sessions that demands that your athletes run more than 350m since anaerobic power contributions to sprinting become negligible after this distance.

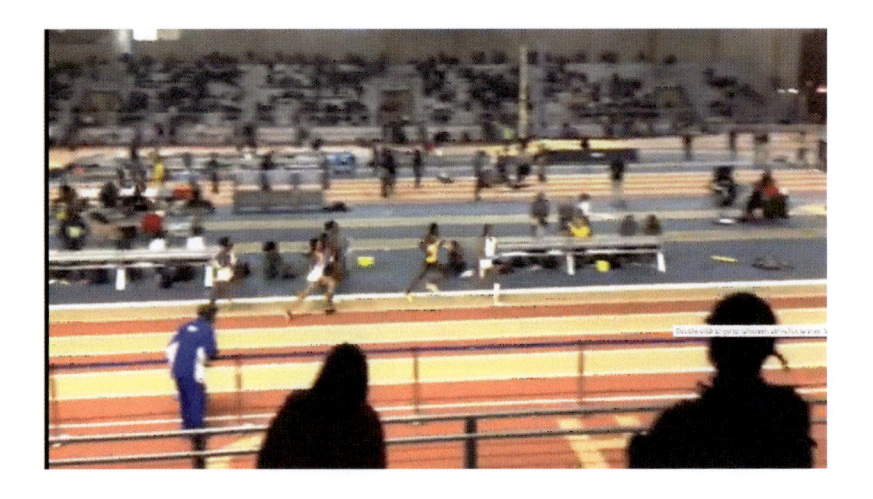

V. Considerations in Training for Speed
Inverted Pyramid Model Progression for Sprint Training

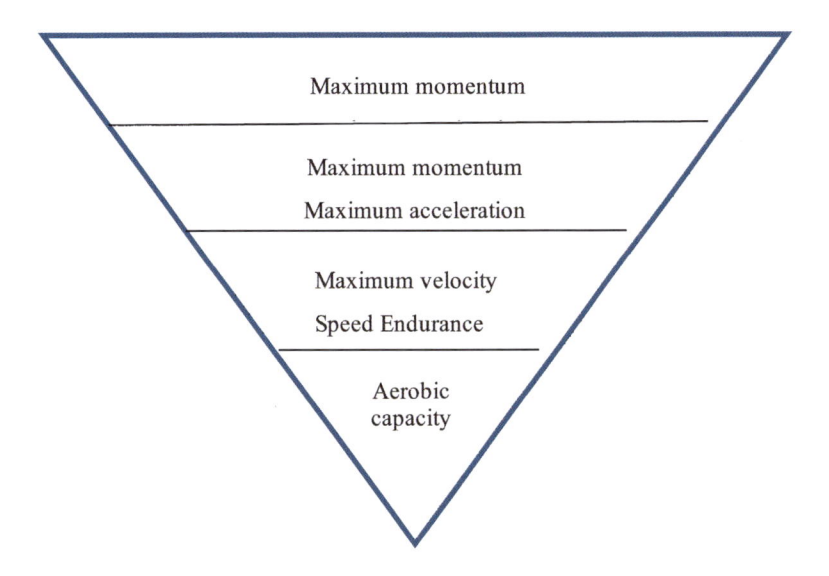

```
Maximum momentum

Maximum momentum
Maximum acceleration

Maximum velocity
Speed Endurance

Aerobic
capacity
```

When training athletes to run faster, ***speed training starts on day one*** (Thomas & Mangiacotti, 2014). When developing maximum speed in your athletes, initially start with block starts of 10-meter runs. All runs are performed at 100% intensity effort. Focus on developing the proper skill techniques needed for drive-phase biomechanical movements and acceleration. Set timing marks for your athletes to meet for all sprint distances during speed sessions. Once your athletes demonstrate proficiency in short distances (10-15m), gradually transition them into longer sprint distances, emphasizing that they maintain proper sprint mechanics (Veney, 2015). Repeated high-intensity runs are necessary to develop maximum speed in your athletes. Proper speed development in your athletes will never be achieved in an environment of fatigue. This means they should have quality runs at maximal or slightly submaximal (95-100%) output efforts. To prevent fatigue and, thus, loss of maximum effort, it is best to train speed over short distances, e.g., 10 to 70 meters at 100% maximum output (Enroth, 2020). To ensure each run is of maximum quality, give athletes enough rest between each rep and set. The accepted rule is that for every 1 second spent in a maximum velocity run, allow 1 minute of rest before beginning another sprint run (Haugen et al., 2019). Longer-intensity runs will require longer rest intervals (Ava, 2011). When training for speed endurance (80-200m), keep session volumes low. This reduces the potential for injury (hamstring, quad, and shin) and CNS fatigue (Bott, 2015; Francis et al., 2019) during a training session. Low-volume sessions also maximize the quality of the runs while minimizing poor biomechanical efforts. Until your athletes master the core foundations for fast running, they will never realize their maximum speed potential. Keep in mind that most youth athletes will take a few years before they approach proficiency in proper biomechanical runs, so be patient. Just remember, you cannot get athletes to run fast if you practice running them slow (Schexnayder, 2011).

When designing training programs, your focus must be on speed/power workouts that use submaximal/maximal runs (intensive training) or quality runs. Quality runs build a *speed muscle strength memory*, allowing athletes to reach competitive speed readiness faster than normal when they return to competition after the offseason (Nuell et al., 2020). To develop increasing speed in athletes, spend more practice time addressing the speed, strength, and power aspects of running and not general training. General training is low-intensity running that includes medium to long runs at a controlled tempo pace. This is the structure of the *short to long sprint training program*, the "inverted pyramid" (Thomas, 2011; Veney, 2011). From my many years spent studying and evaluating peer-reviewed research on sprint performance, I believe the short- to long-sprint training program is the most efficient method of developing speed and speed endurance in youth and high school athletes.

Table (2)

Guidelines for Training Energy Systems

Legend	Anaerobic ATP	Anaerobic ATP-CP Lactate	Anaerobic-Aerobic Glycolate	Aerobic
Duration Time	0-7 secs	7-37 secs	37-40 secs	Hours
Training Distance	10m–70m	80m–250m	50m/ 80m/320m (intervals)	200m–300m (intervals)
Intensity	Maximal (100%)	90–94%	88-92%	70% – 75%
Repetitions	4–8	1–4	2-6	5–10
Recovery (Btw reps)	Full Recovery	4-15 min.; Full recovery	45 secs/90 secs/9' btw rep	90–120 sec
# Sets	1–2	1–2	1–5	1–3
Recovery btw sets	Full Recovery	6-30 min	4/8/20 min	5-6 min

VI. Phases of the Sprint Run

The Start: Momentum Development

The start initiates the drive phase (momentum) of the sprint run and is both a powerful and aggressive event. Simply stated, momentum is the quantity of motion gained by a moving object (Vyas, 2023). **Momentum** (p) is mathematically expressed as the mass (m) multiplied by the velocity (v),

$$(1)\ p = mv$$

At time zero (t_0) of the sprint run, there is no velocity component; therefore, how does the athlete initiate the sprint run to achieve maximum velocity? Consider the following: if the mass (m) is constant throughout the sprint run, then m = K, and the equation (1) becomes

$$(2)\ p = Kv$$

suggesting that strong momentum forces at the start of the run lead to increasing velocities during the sprint run. From Newton's second law (Britannica, 2023) of motion, force equals mass times acceleration (a),

$$(3) \quad f = ma$$

rearranging equation (3),

$$(4) \quad m = f/a,$$

substituting equation (4) into equation (1),

$$(5) \quad p = vf/a$$

At time zero (t_0), there is no acceleration, velocity, or momentum. At the initial start of the sprint run time t_i, speed factors a and v contributions to momentum are negligible, and the development of momentum at the initiation of the sprint run is solely influenced by the application of force that the runner can apply to the ground surface,

$$(6) \quad p \sim f$$

From physics, we know that **power** (P) equals force times velocity (Power, 2019).

$$(7) \quad (P) = fv, \text{ then at } t_i,$$

$$(8) \quad (P) \sim f \sim p \text{ (negligible velocity)}$$

When pushing out of the blocks, athletes should concentrate their efforts on forcibly pushing down and back towards the track through the first 10 to 20 meters of the run. Do not focus too much on how fast they are running. When teaching developing athletes to properly push from a dead start at the beginning of the run, they will often tell you, "This does not feel right," or "I feel like I am running too slow." To effectively achieve maximum velocity later in the run, the athlete initially should explode out of the blocks with such a force that the athlete will achieve a "triple extension" of the body, down from the neck, through the shoulders, down through the hips, and extending downward through the ankles (Musa, 2016).

Triple Extension

An explosive push and step from the blocks will result in the athlete's ability to generate greater initial momentum forces. The results from this push will generally align the athlete's body in a triple extension pattern once they have completely cleared the blocks. Athletes must develop sufficient muscle mass to increase their capacity to apply force to the ground. Increased muscle mass will result in increased momentum production (McErlain-Naylor & Beato, 2021). Increasing momentum at the beginning of a sprint run leads to faster velocities down the track. Athletes can increase their ability to apply force to the ground by increasing their power capacity. Incorporate into your training programs sessions where your athletes do 25-meter sprint runs using overload resistance and release harness belts as well as 30-meter sled pushes.

For muscle mass improvements, schedule Olympic weight training exercises like Romanian deadlifts, power cleans, clean and press, and squats into a regular strength training program (Haugen et al., 2019).

Studies have shown that by combining Olympic weight training with plyometric jumps in circuit fashion, more dramatic effects on sprint performance are realized (Barr, 2014). Getting your athletes on a routine Olympic lift program will increase the power output in their running, and they will see improvements in their ability to forcibly push out of the blocks. To minimize injury and other physical anomalies associated with varying growth rates, youth should not begin weight training until age fourteen.

As a caution, be mindful of over-weight training. Overtraining with weights may increase the athletes overall body mass. Too much gain in body mass may limit maximum velocity potentials, resulting in negative sprint performances over time in your athletes (Mathisen & Pettersen, 2015). Champion sprinters tend to have physiques that exhibit lean weight/height body ratios (Mathisen & Petterson, 2015). From my years of training youth sprinters, in my opinion, the ideal ratio factors of weight to height (wt. in lb. / height in inches) for competitive high school sprinters is 2.20-2.48 for male athletes and 1.79-2.07 for female athletes.

VII. Acceleration and Maximum Velocity

Athletes must have sufficient power to overcome the initial inertia of gravity at the beginning of the sprint run (Kiikka, 2019a). The greater the force your athletes can apply to the track, the greater the momentum, resulting in an extended acceleration phase (Mero, 1988; Morin et al., 2011). Teach your athletes the "falling start" drill (Hall, 2015) so they will learn to effectively push down and back out of the blocks, creating enough force to achieve maximum momentum.

Falling Start

To develop an effective acceleration phase in your athletes, use the falling start drill to create sprint training regimes that:

- Have athletes do acceleration runs over short distances, 10 and 20 meters. When proficiency is achieved, increase training over longer distances,

e.g., 30, and 40 meters, while maintaining 100% levels of run intensity (Mac, 1997).
- For most high school and younger athletes, the acceleration phase is somewhere between 10 to 40 meters (Kiikka, 2019a).
- For athletes 12 years and older, incorporate momentum/acceleration training with starting blocks on day one when sprint training sessions begin.
- If your athletes accelerate properly, they can achieve maximum velocity.

Maximum velocity is the highest possible velocity a runner can reach in a specific period over a distance before biomechanical rhythm is lost due to physiological energy depletion from the runner's metabolic pathway systems (Veney, 2015). Athletes must repeatedly increase force production to the ground over short periods with minimum braking forces to achieve maximum velocity (Morin et al.).

- Develop training regimes that demand that your athletes run fast during practice sessions. The faster your athlete can run, the faster they can run when performing at sub-maximal efforts.

- As discussed earlier in Section II, maximum velocity will be reached for all runners before 7 seconds. Therefore, design maximum velocity training workout programs over distances that your athletes can cover up to 7 seconds (e.g., 4 x 40m, 5 x 50m, 5 x 60m, 5 x 70m). Allow full recovery between all maximum velocity runs.
- Incorporate 30-meter fly runs into your training regimes every 10 training sessions to develop faster velocities in your athletes (Griggs, 2016). To execute the 30-meter fly run use a 25-meter acceleration zone then time the next 30- meters. The total distance is 55-meters. Make sure you record your athletes performances to monitor improvements.
- Please make note that even for world-class sprinters, maximum velocity outputs can only be held for about 30 meters (Coh & Mackala, 2013)
- Preferably, the maximum velocity training session volume should never exceed 450m (Griggs, 2016).

VIII. Considerations for the 400-meter Dash

The 400-meter dash is a high-intensity, demanding event that puts the body under intense stress, fatigue, and pain (Hart, 2012). When running the 400-meter event, the athlete will begin to experience muscle tightening around 250 to 320 meters, causing reduced sprint performance. This is due to the body's inability to remove lactate fast enough during anaerobic glycolysis. Anaerobic glycolysis increases the hydrogen ion concentration, lowering the muscles' pH and reducing the potential for muscle contraction (Patterson, n.d.). The end result is a decrease in the athlete's velocity.

From my years of training athletes to run the 400-meter dash, I recommend that you NEVER HAVE YOUR ATHLETES DO 400-METER RUNS AT COMPETITIVE RACE PACE IN PRACTICE! Using high-intensity 400-meter runs in training sessions teaches your athletes to associate pain with the 400m event. Many youth athletes may avoid the 400-meter dash because they associate pain with the event, even though they have a natural intrinsic ability to excel at it. A good strategy for training youth for the 400m dash is to never allow your athletes to run more than 350-meters (preferably, 300m to 320m) during any high intensity training session. After each endurance run, have your athletes walk around the track as long as needed (do not let them sit down!) until their breathing pattern comes back to normal (full recovery). Refrain from having your athletes perform intensive runs of more than 350 meters during training sessions. (See specific and special endurance in later sections)

Training the athlete's ability to maintain elevated levels of speed for prolonged periods is called Specific Endurance and Special Endurance.

- Specific Endurance (SE): high-intensity runs (92-100% effort) from 150 to 250 meters is used to train athletes to develop speed endurance (Veney, 2011).
- Special Endurance/Lactate (SPE): high-intensity (92-95% effort) runs from 250-350 meters, especially for CNS development and lactate tolerance (Shaver, 2008).
- Incorporate strength training in your 400m sessions that includes short hops, bounds, and a weightlifting regime (Miguel & Reis, 2004).

Note that athletes who struggle in the last 80 meters of the 400m dash do so because (1) they have not run enough repeated 320-meter high-intensity runs in practice sessions. Such practice distances allow the CNS to adapt to the intense physiological demands while under stress during the run, and (2) the athlete has not done enough aerobic tempo runs in general practice session training (Thomas, 2012).

Teach your athletes how to run (race modeling) the 400-meter dash by having them focus on hitting the timing marks set for the workout distances during your training regimes each session. If workouts are designed properly, the athlete's workout sessions should model the actual 400-meter race. Once your athletes become proficient in their 400-meter training, they will have learned that the first 300 meters is an all-out sprint at close to 90% maximum velocity. Although their velocities will significantly decrease during the lactate phase of the run (280-330 meters), their aerobic endurance training should position them to finish strong for the final 80–100 meters of the race.

When doing aerobic endurance training with sprinters, try to schedule these training sessions apart from sprint and power-related activities if possible. *Never* combine speed training and aerobic endurance training in the same session (Schexnayder, 2011). Schedule training workouts that use interval training to develop aerobic capacity in your athletes when doing extensive training sessions (recovery days). Interval training will preserve proper mechanics in your athletes while allowing for recovery of injuries that may occur during a state of fatigue during intensive training sessions.

Tempo runs (extensive training), a form of interval training, are best suited for athletes during endurance sessions and are most favorable for aerobic conditioning. Tempo running workouts like the 200-meter repeat (Hart, 2012) and 50-meter repeat allow your athletes to maintain efficient sprint mechanics, proper breathing techniques, improve cardiovascular health, and an understanding of race modeling. For 400-meter athletes, it is recommended that tempo runs of 200 or 300 meters be performed at a 70% to 75% pace of the athlete's best time in those events (PR). Initially, your athletes will struggle miserably, but over time, they should be able to do 5 reps in one set. Be careful not to over-run your athletes until they fatigue badly! The workouts end when you see continuing mechanical failure during aerobic training (Ava, 2011).

When trained properly, your athletes will have approximately 40 seconds of anaerobic capacity reserves for running the 400-meter dash. Running at 90% maximum velocity, the goal of the 400-meter runner is to cover as much of the 400-meter distance as possible in 40 seconds. Elite high school male and female sprinters can cover about 345 meters and 310 meters, respectively, in 40 seconds. Most athletes 12 years old or younger can cover about 200-275 meters during this time period. After 40 seconds, the strength of the athletes aerobic endurance training will decide how strongly they finish the race. Years of observing youth track performances strongly suggest that the aerobic energy contribution for the 400-meter dash is more significant in youth athletes (12 years or younger) than in older, physiologically developed athletes. Adjust your workout regimes to include more aerobic capacity sessions when training athletes 12 years and under for the 400-meter dash. As your athletes age into their teen years, you will begin to observe that continuing high volumes of aerobic training regimes will result in minimal gains for decreasing 400-meter times.

From my almost thirty years as a youth track and field coach, using 100-meter times (FAT) as a base for calculations, my data (not published) strongly suggest that for elite 100-meter male high school sprinters ($\leq$ 10.60s) who also run the 400-meter dash ($\leq$ 48.5s), their anaerobic energy contribution is about 71% and their aerobic energy contribution about 29%. Thus, the 400-meter dash is a sprint! Male world-class quarter milers will turn the 300 meters between 30.8 and 31.5 seconds, and females between 35.5 and 37.0 seconds! Therefore, if your athletes are to be competitive in the 400-meter event, they will have to develop fast front-end speed potential.

<u>When training youth athletes to achieve maximum speed potential, allow them to run as fast and as far as they can until you observe mechanical breakdown.</u> When mechanics fail, the quality of speed training runs will not be enhanced, and normal braking forces will begin to influence the outcome of the sprint run. Do not allow athletes to run with poor mechanics during the progression of a training workout. When observing continuing mechanical breakdown in your athletes during speed or speed endurance practice sessions, terminate the remaining workouts in the training session (Ava, 2011). Always remember when developing sprinters for elite competition, make sure you design running workouts that consist primarily of speed training.

IX. Considerations for Speed Workouts (Event Specific Training)

Maximum Volume Ranges per Session

Speed

100m dash/100mh	300-480m
200m dash	400-600m
400m dash	400-900m

Speed Endurance

100m/100mh	N/A
200m	700-800m
400m/400mh	700-900m

Special Endurance

400m	900-1400m
400m	900-1400m

Aerobic Endurance

400m	1000-1800m
400mh	1400-2400m

*mh-hurdles

Warm-Up Drills and Calisthenics

(Note: Proper warm-up is a minimum of 25 minutes, and the distance should be 30 meters unless noted otherwise.)

Right-over-left and Left-over-right Stretch
Hurdle Stretch (left and right legs)
High Hops (20 meters)
Across the Front Arm Swing Skips (30 meters)
Forward Arm Swing Skips (30 meters)
Backward Arm Swing Skips
Reaching Back Leg Runs (30 meters)
Butterflies
Karaoke
Straight-Leg Bounds (50 meters)
Alternating Leg Bound Jumps
1-2-3 Stretch
Ankle Turns
Full Ankle Turns
Toe Walks
Dyno Walks
Basketball Shuffle (if it is warm)
Hamstring Walks (Tin Man Walks)
Groin Walks
A-Skip
B-Skip
C-Skip
Backwards C-Skip
Fast Leg (right leg) Runs
Fast Leg (left leg) Runs
Alternating Fast Leg Runs

X. Sample Training Sessions

ATP-Energy System (Speed)

Mon	Tues	Wed	Thurs	Friday
8 x 40m intervals @ 4' min btw runs @ 100%	3 x 10m 3 x 20m 3 x 30m 3 x 50m @ 100%; Full recovery	wicket drill; 3 x 30m, fly runs; 60m; Full recovery	drills, agility, hill running; weight training	6 x 60m or 6 x 80m @ 100%, Full recovery

ATP-Creatine Phosphate (Speed Endurance)

Mon	Tues	Wed	Thurs	Friday
6 x 150m sprint repeats @ 90%; 6' btw runs	wicket drill, bound drills	1 x 150; 9' 1 x 120; 6' 1 x 75; 4' 1 x 50 @ 90%	6 x 120m @ 90%, 5' btw runs	4 x 120m @ 95% full recovery

Specific Endurance [SE]

Mon	Tues	Wed	Thurs	Friday
2 x 6 x 80m sprint repeats @ 90%; 3' btw runs; 8' btw sets	1 x 250; 10' 1 x 180; 8' 1 x 150; 6' 1 x 120 @ 92%,	wicket drill. bound drills	3 x 250m @ 90%; 12'	4 x 150m @ 92% full recovery btw runs

Aerobic Capacity

Mon	Tues	Wed	Thurs	Friday
1 x 5 x 200m; 1x3 x 200m Repeats @ 75% 90"- 2' btw runs, 5' btw sets	warm-up stretch	2-3 broken 400m @ 75%, 1' btw 200'; 5' btw sets	4 x 5 x 50-meter intervals. sprint 50m @ 80%, jog back 50m - repeat; 5' recovery btw sets	drill day

Special Endurance – Lactate [SPE]

Mon	Tues	Wed	Thurs	Friday
1 x 350m/1 x 320m @ 90%; 20' btw runs; 2-3 x 150m @ 93%;10' btw runs	30 min hill running @ 100%	4-6 x 150m @ 93%, 12' btw runs	4 x 200m @ 92%, 10' btw runs	4 x 100 @ 93%, 12' btw runs

XI. Considerations for Club Track Training Schedules

Sun	Mon	Tues	Wed	Thurs	Fri	Sat
Month 1	Pre-Competitive Season Over Distance Training					
Month 2	100m-400m Anaerobic-[ATP/ATP-CP] { block starts}					
Month 3	100m/200m Anaerobic-[ATP/ATP-CP] {block starts} Season starts, (400m) Interval training: high school 10% (youth 30%)					
Month 4	100m/200m-100% Anaerobic-[ATP/ATP-CP]; (400m)- 75% -[ATP/ATP-CP]; 15% SE-SPE; interval training: high school 10% (youth 30%)					
Month 5	100m/200m-100% Anaerobic-[ATP/ATP-CP]; (400m) 55% [ATP/ATP-CP]; 20 % SE-SPE Lactate Aerobic training-25% (youth 35-40%)					
Month 6	100m/200m - 100% Anaerobic-[ATP/ATP-CP] (400m) 45% -[ATP/ATP-CP]; 25% SE-SPE Lactate; 30% Aerobic-tempo runs (youth 35-40%)					
Month 7	100m/200m - 100% Anaerobic-[ATP/ATP-CP] (400m) 45% -[ATP/ATP-CP]; 25% SE-SPE Lactate; 30% Aerobic-tempo runs (youth 35-40%)					
	AAU National Meet					

7-Month Club Track Season

Considerations for High School Track and Field

Sun	Mon	Tues	Wed	Thurs	Fri	Sat
Month 1	Anaerobic-[ATP/ATP-CP {block starts}] Speed					
Month 2	Season starts, 100m-200m Anaerobic-[ATP/ATP-CP {block starts}]; (400m) 90%-[ATP/ATP-CP] {block starts}; 10%-Aerobic training, Interval training: tempo runs					
Month 3	100m-200m Anaerobic-[ATP/ATP-CP {block starts}] (400m)-60% -[ATP/ATP-CP]; 15% SE-SPE Lactate; 25% Aerobic training: tempo runs					
Month 4	100m/200m-100% Anaerobic-[ATP/ATP-CP] (400m) 45%-[ATP/ATP-CP]; 25%-SE-SPE Lactate; 30% Aerobic-Interval training: tempo runs					

4-Month High School Season

XII. Glossary of Definitions

Acceleration: the rate of change of velocity or how quickly an athlete can increase the velocity of the motion.

Aerobics: metabolic energy production in the presence of oxygen.

Anaerobic: metabolic energy production in the absence of oxygen.

ATP (adenosine triphosphate): the organic molecule that provides energy to support and sustain biological processes like muscle contraction in living organisms.

Backside Mechanics: The push-back of the legs to the ground when sprinting.

Biomechanical: The Kinetics and Kinematics of motion as it relates to running.

Braking forces: The horizontal forces that push back on the leg when the foot makes contact with the ground.

Capacity: the maximum amount of energy that a living organism can produce.

Cardiovascular: the circulatory system of the heart and blood vessels, which carry nutrients and oxygen throughout the body.

Central nervous system: the complex of nerves that run from the brain and spinal cord that controls the body's sensory motor responses.

Coordination: the ability to perform multiple smooth movements into a single fluid movement.

Core: the central part of your body, encompassing your stomach, lower back, hips, and pelvis areas.

Creatine Phosphate: a biochemical compound that is stored in the skeletal-muscular network that, when released, converts ADP to ATP.

Dynamics: the study of the motion of bodies under the application of force.

Endurance: the capacity to express high-speed runs over an extended period of time.

Energetics: a discipline of science that is concerned with how energy is utilized in chemical, biological, and physical processes.

Ergo-dynamics: the study or evaluation of the body's entire range of motion while running.

Extensive training: a range of large volumes of moderate-paced running designed to increase aerobic capacity.

Fast-twitch muscle fibers: muscles that operate without the need for oxygen, contract easily, and release the most energy but rapidly fatigue.

Fatigue: lack of energy reserves resulting from mental or physical exertion.

Front Side Mechanics: Using proper leg and pelvis alignment when sprinting.

Intensive training: high-intensity running performed with a maximum or submaximal effort that requires ample rest to repeat performance.

Kinematics: the study of the motion of objects without regard to the forces that cause the motion.

Lactate: a condition or state of lack of oxygen and the production of H protons in muscle tissue.

Locomotion: the displacement of a body from one place to another.

Mass: anything that can be weighted.

Maximal: the upper or higher limit.

Maximum velocity: the highest rate of speed an athlete can attain.

Mechanics: the description, detailed analysis, and assessment of human movement during sports activities.

Medium-twitch muscle fibers: similar to fast-twitch muscle but much lower in ATP content and contain the metabolic potential to use oxygen for energy production.

Momentum: the amount of motion that a moving body creates, measured as a product of its mass and velocity.

Muscles: organs consisting of fibrous tissues that have the ability to shorten or lengthen to produce motion.

Neurobiology: branch of science that studies the anatomy, physiology, and pathology of the nervous system.

Neuromuscular: the motor skill relationships between the nerves and muscles.

Physiology: A branch of biology that describes the chemistry and functions of body parts in living organisms.

Slow-twitch muscle fibers: fatigue-resistant muscles that are efficient at using oxygen to produce ATP needed to cause muscle contractions over extended periods of time.

Speed: the ability of the neuromuscular system to produce the greatest possible impulse in the shortest possible time through a specified distance.
Submaximal: energy output less than the maximum output that the athlete is capable of producing.

Supramaximal: working at an intensity higher than what is generally required.

Tempo running runs at a sustained pace that is appreciably slower than your maximum output.

Velocity: the speed of an object as it moves in one direction

References

Ava. (2011, November 10). *PPT - Shelia Burrell Sprints, Hurdles, Jumps Coach Georgetown University Washington, DC PowerPoint Presentation - ID:193589*. SlideServe. https://www.slideserve.com/Ava/shelia-burrell-sprints-hurdles-jumps-coach-georgetown-university-washington-dc

Barr, M. J. (2014). *A Series of Studies Examining the Development of Sprint Speed and Momentum of International Rugby Union Players*. Edith Cowan University.

Bott, C. (2015, August). *Central Nervous System Fatigue: Effects on Speed, Power, and Athletes*. SimpliFaster. https://simplifaster.com/articles/central-nervous-system-fatigue-effects-speed-power-athletes/

Britannica. (2023). Newton's laws of motion - Newton's second law: F = ma. *Encyclopedia Britannica*. https://www.britannica.com/science/Newtons-laws-of-motion/Newtons-second-law-F-ma

Brown, T. D., & Vescovi, J. D. (2012). Maximum Speed. *Strength and Conditioning Journal*, 34(2), 37–41. https://doi.org/10.1519/ssc.0b013e31824ea156

Chavez, M. (2023, September 30). *Youth Strength Training*. Science for Sport. https://www.scienceforsport.com/youth-strength-training/

Coh, M., & Mackala, K. (2013). Differences between the elite and sub-elite sprinters in kinematic and dynamic determinations of countermovement jump and drop jump. *Journal of Strength and Conditioning Research*, 27(11), 3021–3027. https://doi.org/10.1519/JSC.0b013e31828c14d8

Elsevier. (2016). *The physics of sports. Elsevier Connect.*
https://www.elsevier.com/connect/the-physics-of-sports

Enroth, M. (2020). *100-Meter Sprint Running: Event Analysis and Programming of Training and Coaching.* University of Jyväskylä, JYX Digital Repository.
https://jyx.jyu.fi/handle/123456789/71379

Fletcher, I. (2008). *Biomechanical Principles in Sprint Running. Ariel Dynamics.*
https://www1.macrosport.com/start/apas/studies/Biomechanics_of_Sprinting_-_Fletcher.pdf

Francis, C., Smith, J., Tellez, T., Phelps S. M., Pfaff D., & Kersee B. (2011, March 6). *Complete Sprinting Technique.* AdrianSprints.com.
http://www.adriansprints.com/2011/03/complete-sprinting-technique-charlie.html

Griggs, R. (2016). *Keys to Developing Combo 400m/800m Runner (CTF Clinic).* Complete Track and Field.

Hall, B. (2015). *Falling Starts Speed Drill* [Video]. YouTube.
https://www.youtube.com/watch?v=1SwGCdVWRZ0

Hart, C. (2012). *400m/800m Training Program.* Championship Productions.

Haugen, T., Seiler, S., Sandbakk, Ø., & Tønnessen, E. (2019). The Training and Development of Elite Sprint Performance: An Integration of Scientific and Best Practice Literature. *Sports Medicine.* 5(1).
https://doi.org/10.1186/s40798-019-0221-0

Hiserman, J. (2009). *A Total Sprint-Training Program for Maximum Strength, Power, Sprint Speed, & Core Strength.* Speed Endurance.
https://speedendurance.com/2009/04/19/a-total-sprint-training-program-for-maximum-strength-power-sprint-speed-core-strength/

Kiikka, D. (2019a). *Acceleration in Sports-The Key to Athletic Success*. The Sports Edu. https://thesportsedu.com/acceleration-definition/

Kiikka D. (2019b). *Power in Sports and Athletic Performance- And Why We Need It*. The Sports Edu. https://thesportsedu.com/power-in-sports/

Lacquaniti, F., Ivanenko, Y. P., & Zago, M. (2012). Development of Human Locomotion. *Current Opinion in Neurobiology, 22*(5), 822-828.

Mac, B. (1997). *100-metres Training*. Brian Mac Sports Coach. https://www.brianmac.co.uk/sprints/tp100.htm

Mathisen, G., & Pettersen, S. A. (2015). Anthropometric factors related to sprint and agility performance in young male soccer players. *Open Access Journal of Sports Medicine*, 337. https://doi.org/10.2147/oajsm.s91689

Nuell, S., Illera-Domínguez, V. R., Carmona, G., Alomar, X., Padullés, J. M., Lloret, M., & Cadefau, J. A. (2020). Hypertrophic muscle changes and sprint performance enhancement during a sprint-based training macrocycle in national-level sprinters. *European Journal of Sports Science, 20*(6), 793–802. https://doi.org/10.1080/17461391.2019.1668063

Osar, E. (2015, April 14). *Frontal Plane Exercises for Improving Speed and Agility*. Athletes Acceleration. https://athletesacceleration.com/frontal-plane-exercise-for-improving-speed-and-agility/

Patterson, K. (n.d.). Chemistry and Sport - Athletics: 400m. RSC Education. https://edu.rsc.org/resources/chemistry-and-sport-athletics-400m/857.article

Power. (n.d.). The Physics Classroom. https://www.physicsclassroom.com/class/energy/Lesson-1/Power

Quaal, R. (2019, July 7). *What Athletes Need to Know About the Nervous System*. Stack. https://www.stack.com/a/lift-or-rest-it-depends-on-your-nervous-system/

Sawka, M. N., Wenger, C. B., Young, A. J., & Pandolf, K. B. (1993). *Physiological Responses to Exercise in the Heat*. Nutritional Needs in Hot Environments - NCBI Bookshelf. https://www.ncbi.nlm.nih.gov/books/NBK236240/

Schexnayder, B. (2011). *Developing Speed in High School Athletes*. Complete Track and Field.

Seagrave, L. (1996). *Introduction to Sprinting*. IAAF.

Seagrave, L., Mouchbahani, R., & O'Donnell, K. (2011, October 10). *Neuro-Biomechanics of Maximum Velocity Sprinting*. Complete Track and Field. https://completetrackandfield.com/wp-content/uploads/2011/01/Maximum_Velocity_Sprinting.pdf

Settle, Leo. (2014). *Developing Speed: A Neurological Approach*. Coaches Insider. https://coachesinsider.com/track-x-country/developing-speed-a-neurological-approach-article/

Shaver, D. (2008). *Spring Training*. 18th NACACTFCA International Athletic Conference.

Smith, J. (2019). *Nervous System Training 101: The Creation of Superhumans Strength and Athleticism*. Train Heroic. https://www.trainheroic.com/blog/nervous-system-training-101-the-creation-of-superhuman-strength-and-athleticism/

Stergiou, N., Blanke, D., Myers, S. A., & Siu, K. C. (2016). *Introduction to Exercise Science: 4th Edition.* DigitalCommons@UNO. https://digitalcommons.unomaha.edu/biomechanicsbooks/2

Teichmann, J., Burchardt, H., Tan, R. L., & Healy, P. D. (2021). Hip Mobility and Flexibility for Track and Field Athletes. *Advances in Physical Education, 11*(02), 221–231. https://doi.org/10.4236/ape.2021.112017

Thomas, L. (2011). *The 3 Laws of Speed Development.* Complete Track and Field.

Thomas, L. (2012). *3 Reasons Why Sprinters Fall Apart at the End of The Race.* Complete Track and Field.

Thomas, L. (2014). *Complete Speed Training 3.* Complete Track and Field.

Thomas, L., & Mangiacotti, M. (2014). *Speed Training Starts Early.* Complete Track and Field.

Thompson, P. (1991). The Energy Systems. *Introduction to Coaching Theory* (pp. 79-82). IAAF.

Thorson, M. (2018). *Marauder Speed "Getting You There Faster.* Track and Field News. https://trackandfieldnews.com/track-coach/marauder-speed-getting-you-there-faster/

Tottori, N., Suga, T., Miyake, Y., Tsuchikane, R., Tanaka, T., Terada, M., Otsuka, M., Nagano, A., Fujita, S., & Isaka, T. (2021). Trunk and lower limb muscularity in sprinters: what are the specific muscles for superior sprint performance? *BMC Research Notes, 14*(1). https://doi.org/10.1186/s13104-021-05487-x

Trappe, S., Luden, N. D., Minchev, K., Raue, U., Jemioło, B., & Trappe, T. A. (2015). Skeletal Muscle Signature of a Champion Sprint Runner. *Journal of Applied Physiology, 118*(12), 1460-1466. https://doi.org/10.1152/japplphysiol.00037.2015

U.S. Energy Information Administration. (2022, December 27). *What is energy? Explained - U.S. energy information administration (EIA)*. Eia.gov. https://www.eia.gov/energyexplained/what-is-energy/

Vella C. A., & Kravitz, L. (2004). *Staying Cool When Your Body Is Hot*. AKWA.

Veney, T. (2011). *Sprint Training-Energy Systems*. Complete Track and Field.

Veney, T. (2015). *An Introduction to Conditioning Sprint and Hurdles*. Complete Track and Field.

Vyas, K. (2023, June 26). *Momentum in Physics: Newton's Laws of Motion and Collisions*. Interesting Engineering. https://interestingengineering.com/science/momentum-in-physics-newtons-laws-of-motion-collisions-and-more

Yang, F., Espy, D., & Pai, Y. C. (2009). Feasible stability region in the frontal plane during human gait. *Annals of Biomedical Engineering, 37*(12), 2606–2614. https://doi.org/10.1007/s10439-009-9798-7

Young, M. (2007). *Maximal Velocity Sprint Mechanics* [Video]. YouTube. https://www.youtube.com/watch?v=tiLeM6STHXI

Young, M. (2013, November 18). Maximal Velocity Sprint Mechanics. EliteTrack. https://www.elitetrack.com/articles/articles-read-2341/

Printed in Great Britain
by Amazon